Famous Business Quotes And Sayings Pocket Book By Subject

By BMVDFUND

Put this book on your pocket.
Read, Understood, Remember It And Do Something.
The bibe of business operate.
All aspects of business life.
Bedside book of businessman.

Copyright 2014

ISBN-13:

978-1502784919

ISBN-10:

1502784912

Contents

Introduction

This book is usual quotes book as you seen in many quotes on internet.
Because the quotes in it was selectived and arranged with subjects business.
All the quotes or sayings was applied on my business and my life.
So that I love it as my life. I removed thousand of quotes that I feel useless
or not realistic to made this book. I want it become a the bibe of business
operations and a bedside book of every businessman in the world.

Althought, these quotes was not said by me but I only choose the quotes I
love and I think it is value. I try to cheapest I can so that more people can
reach it, especially for someone who passion for success. I took 6 years to
completed this book and I hope it bring you new ideas and knowledge for
your business and your life. Anyone, from normal person, to students or
professional, I think you must read it to make you better and better.
Happy Reading!
M-Trader

Chapter : Money

Money without brains is always dangerous.
Napoleon Hill

Rich people manage their money well. Poor people mismanage their money well.
T.Harv Eker

We go to school to learn to work hard for money. I write books and create products that teach people how to have money work hard for them.
Robert Kiyosaki

The lack of money is the root of all evil.
Mark Twain

Money is a singular thing. It ranks with love as man's greatest source of joy. And with death as his greatest source of anxiety. Over all history it has oppressed nearly all people in one of two ways: either it has been abundant and very unreliable, or reliable and very scarce.
John Kenneth Galbraith

He that is of the opinion money will do everything may well be suspected of doing everything for money.
Benjamin Franklin

Money is like an arm or leg -- use it or lose it.
Henry Ford

A Penny Saved is a Penny Earned
Benjamin Franklin

You can be young without money but you can't be old without it.
Tennessee Williams

God gave me my money. I believe the power to make money is a gift from God . to be developed and used to the best of our ability for the good of mankind. Having been endowed with the gift I possess, I believe it is my duty to make money and still more money and to use the money I make for the good of my fellow man according to the dictates of my conscience.

John D Rockefeller

The importance of money flows from it being a link between the present and the future.
John Maynard Keynes

I know of nothing more despicable and pathetic than a man who devotes all the hours of the waking day to the making of money for money's sake.
John D Rockefeller

If you can count your money, you don't have a billion dollars.
J. Paul Getty

Time is money.
Benjamin Franklin

Money was never a big motivation for me, except as a way to keep score. The real excitement is playing the game.
Donald Trump

Money alone sets all the world in motion.
Publilius Syrus

Never spend your money before you have it.
Thomas Jefferson

It's not how much money you make, but how much money you keep, how hard it works for you, and how many generations you keep it for.
Robert Kiyosaki

Money is the opposite of the weather. Nobody talks about it, but everybody does something about it.
Rebecca Johnson

Too many people spend money they haven't earned, to buy things they don't want, to impress people they don't like.
Will Smith

Rich people have their money work hard for them. Poor people work hard for their money.

T.Harv Eker

If money is your hope for independence you will never have it. The only real security that a man will have in this world is a reserve of knowledge, experience, and ability.
Henry Ford

All money means to me is a pride in accomplishment.
Ray Kroc

My favorite things in life don't cost any money. It's really clear that the most precious resource we all have is time.
Steve Jobs

What's money? A man is a success if he gets up in the morning and goes to bed at night and in between does what he wants to do.
Bob Dylan

A wise person should have money in their head, but not in their heart.
Jonathan Swift

Chapter : Rich

It is a bad thing that many from being rich should become poor; for men of ruined fortunes are sure to stir up revolutions.
Aristotle

Rich people are excellent receivers. Poor people are poor receivers.
T. Harv Eker

Political economy tracesinanabstract way theeffects of the desire to be rich; and nations must nowadays abound in that passion if theyare to have much poweror respect in the world.
Walter Bagehot

Rich people believe "I create my life." Poor people believe "Life happens to me."
T. Harv Eker

A rich man told me recently that a liberal is a man who tells other people what to do with their money.
Jones

The rich man's wealth is his strong city: the destruction of the poor is their poverty.
Bible

Rich people have small TVs and big libraries, and poor people have small libraries and big TVs.
Zig Ziglar

Rich people are committed to being rich. Poor people want to be rich.
T.Harv Eker

Laws grind the poor, and rich men rule the law.
Oliver Goldsmith

There's nothing surer, the rich get rich and the poor get children.
Gus Kahn

Rich people are bigger than their problems. Poor people are smaller than their problems.
T.Harv Eker

All wealth is the product of labor.
John Locke

Chapter : Poor

When you are poor, be good to others. Don't be calculative. When you are poor, spend money so that people can see it. When you are poor, spend money on others. When you are poor, spend less time at home and more time outside. When you are poor, you have to throw yourself out in the open and let people make good use of you.
Li Ka Shing

The poor is hated even of his own neighbour: but the rich hath many friends.
Bible

The difference between rich and poor", said Francie, "is that the poor do everything with thier own hands and the rich hire hands to do things.
Betty Smith

Rich people associate with positive, successful people. Poor people associate with negative or unsuccessful people. Rich people constantly learn and grow. Poor people think they already know.
T.Harv Eker

To fight the poverty, we must feel the poverty.
M.F. Moonzajer

Poverty is the parent of revolution and crime.
Aristotle

Rich people are willing to promote themselves and their value. Poor people think negatively about selling and promotion.
T.Harv Eker

Some people think luxury is the opposite of poverty. It is not. It is the opposite of vulgarity.
Coco Chanel

Poor men's reasons are not heard.
Dr. Thomas Fuller

Rich people focus on opportunities. Poor people focus on obstacles. Rich people act in spite of fear. Poor people let fear stop them.

T.Harv Eker

Chapter : Success

The secret of success is to do the common things uncommonly well.
John D. Rockefeller

Successful people are always looking for opportunities to help others.
Unsuccessful people are asking, What's in it for me? –
Brian Tracy

Man must first has aspiration, then has insights and persistence. Aspiration
prevents us from being nasty and obscene.
Li Ka-Shing

The men who have succeeded are men who have chosen one line and stuck
to it.
Andrew Carnegie

To be successful, you have to have your heart in your business, and your
business in your heart.
Thomas J. Watson

Success is not the key to happiness. Happiness is the key to success. If you
love what you are doing, you will be successful.
Albert Schweitzer

Winners never quit and quitters never win.
Vince Lombardi

High expectations are the key to everything.
Sam Walton

It's hard to beat a person who never gives up.
Babe Ruth

As long as you're going to be thinking anyway, think big.
Donald Trump

If opportunity doesn't knock, build a door.
Milton Berle

I'm convinced that about half of what separates the successful entrepreneurs from the non-successful ones is pure perseverance.
Steve Jobs

I never dreamed about success. I worked for it.
Estee Lauder

Success is neither magical nor mysterious. Success is the natural consequence of consistently applying the basic fundamentals.
Jim Rohn

Timing, perseverance, and ten years of trying will eventually make you look like an overnight success.
Biz Stone

There's no mystery in business success. If you do each day's task successfully and stay faithfully within these natural operations of commercial laws which I talk so much about and keep your head clear, you will come out all right.
John D. Rockefeller

The key to success is for you to make a habit throughout your life of doing the things you fear.
Vincent Van Gogh

Chapter : Startup

I don't look to jump over 7-foot bars: I look around for 1-foot bars that I can step over.
Warren Buffet

You may not be a Picasso or Mozart but you don't have to be. Just create to create. Create to remind yourself you're still alive. Make stuff to inspire others to make something too. Create to learn a bit more about yourself.
Frederic Terral

What do you need to start a business? Three simple things: know your product better than anyone, know your customer, and have a burning desire to succeed.
Dave Thomas

Whether you think you can, or think you can't — you're right.
Henry Ford

Chase the vision, not the money; the money will end up following you.
Tony Hsieh

You have to be ready for hard work and frugal spending to get the idea off the ground.
Garrett Camp

Any time is a good time to start a company.
Ron Conway

I knew that if I failed I wouldn't regret that, but I knew the one thing I might regret is not trying.
Jeff Bezos

The way to get started is to quit talking and start doing.
Walt Disney

Act enthusiastic and you will be enthusiastic.
Dale Carnegie

Whatever the mind can conceive and believe, the mind can achieve.

Dr. Napoleon Hill

I don't think an economic slump will hurt good ideas.
Rob Kalin

Your time is limited, so don't waste it living someone else's life.
Steve Jobs

I'm here to build something for the long-term. Anything else is a distraction.
Mark Zuckerberg

When you're ready to quit, you're closer than you think.
Bob Parsons

Live in the future, then build what's missing.
Paul Graham

The best startups generally come from somebody needing to scratch an itch.
Michael Arrington

Fearlessness is like a muscle. I know from my own life that the more I
exercise it the more natural it becomes to not let my fears run me.
Arianna Huffington

Starting your own business is like riding a roller coaster. There are highs and
lows and every turn you take is another twist. The lows are really low, but
the highs can be really high. You have to be strong, keep your stomach tight,
and ride along with the roller coaster that you started.
Lindsay Manseau

Starting a company is like getting married and having a kid.
Matt Brezina

If you believe in something, work nights and weekends, i wont feel like
work.
Kevin Rose

Openly share and talk to people about your idea. Use their lack of interest or doubt to fuel your motivation to make it happen.
Todd Garland

Starting a business is a huge amount of hard work... You had better enjoy it.
Richard Branson

Start small and dream big.
Rich Dad

Chapter: Innovation and Oppotunities

I try not to make any decisions that I'm not excited about.
Jake Nickell

When you innovate, you've got to be prepared for people telling you that you are nuts.
Larry Ellison

Do not follow where the path may lead. Go instead where there is no path and leave a trail.
Ralph Waldo Emerson

Waiting for perfect is never as smart as making progress.
Seth Godin

Innovation distinguishes between a leader and a follower.
Steve Jobs

If you always do what you always did, you will always get what you always got.
Albert Einstein

The best way to predict the future is to invent it.
Alan Kay

A discovery is said to be an accident meeting a prepared mind.
Von Szent-Gyorgyi

The impossible is often the untried.
J. Goodwin

Creativity is thinking up new things. Innovation is doing new things.
Ted Levitt

If you are not willing to risk the unusual, you will have to settle for the ordinary.
Jim Rohn

Just do it..

Nike

You must do the things you think you cannot do.
Eleanor Roosevelt

Learning and innovation go hand in hand. The arrogance of success is to think that what you did yesterday will be sufficient for tomorrow.
William Pollard

What I have dreamed in an hour is worth more than what you have done in four.
Lorenzo de' Medici
Opportunity is missed by most people because it is dressed in overalls and looks like work.
Thomas Edison

We're going where no one has gone before. There's no model to follow, nothing to copy. That is what makes this so exciting.
Richard Branson

Chapter : Ideas

Good ideas are common – what's uncommon are people who'll work hard enough to bring them about.
Ashleigh Brilliant

My ideas usually come not at my desk writing but in the midst of living.
Anais Nin

The ability to convert ideas to things is the secret of outward success.
Henry Ward Beecher

Ideas can be life-changing. Sometimes all you need to open the door is just one more good idea.
Jim Rohn

Everyone who's ever taken a shower has an idea. It's the person who gets out of the shower, dries off and does something about it who makes a difference.
Nolan Bushnell

Human history is, in essence, a history of ideas.
H.G. Wells

Things that annoy me end up fuelling my ideas.
Josh James

If I have a thousand ideas and only one turns out to be good, I am satisfied.
Alfred Bernhard Nobel

The value of an idea lies in the using of it.
Thomas Edison

Everyone is a genius at least once a year. The real geniuses simply have their bright ideas closer together.
Georg Christoph Lichtenberg

Don't worry about people stealing your ideas. If your ideas are any good, you'll have to ram them down people's throats.
Howard Aiken

Ideas are commodity. Execution of them is not.
Michael Dell

Ideas are easy. Implementation is hard.
Guy Kawasaki

I'm always throwing out ideas, so it 's not creativity, it's just volume.
Ben Huh

Ideas are in between strategy and execution
MT Rainey

The way to get good ideas is to get lots of ideas and throw the bad ones away.
Linus Pauling

All achievements, all earned riches, have their beginning in an idea.
Napoleon Hill

It is the essence of genius to make use of the simplest ideas.
Charles Peguy

I know quite certainly that I myself have no special talent. Curiosity, obsession and dogged endurance, combined with self-criticism, have brought me to my ideas.
Albert Einstein

I begin with an idea and then it becomes something else.
Pablo Picasso

Money never starts an idea; it is the idea that starts the money.
William J. Cameron

The man with a new idea is a crank -- until the idea succeeds.
Mark Twain

The great accomplishments of man have resulted from the transmission of ideas of enthusiasm.
Thomas Watson

Our best ideas come from clerks and stockboys.
Sam Walton

Ideas must work through the brains and arms of men, or they are no better than dreams.
Ralph Waldo Emerson

Great minds discuss ideas; Average minds discuss events; Small minds discuss people.
Eleanor Roosevelt

We bring together the best ideas-turning the meetings of our top managers into intellectual orgies.
Jack Welch

A mediocre idea that generates enthusiasm will go farther than a great idea that inspires no one.
Mary Kay Ash

Chapter: Mistakes and Failures

We are not really good at knowing what we want, and we are very quick to say " this sucks". That is where the opportunity lies.
Gary Vaynerchuk

The minute you get away from the fundamentals – whether it's proper technique, work ethic, or mental preparation – the bottom can fall out of your game.
Michael Jordan

No person will make a great business who wants to do it all himself or get all the credit.
Andrew Carnegie

Don't make decisions based on fear.
Jake Nickell

If you're going through hell, keep going.
Winston Churchill

Don't compromise what you wouldn't want for a quick buck.
Noah Everett

Observe the world around you everything you do, and especially everything you hate to do.
Aaron Patzer

We cannot solve a problem by using the same kind of thinking we used when we created them.
Einstein

Experience is the name everyone gives to their mistakes.
Oscar Wilde

Anyone who has never made a mistake has never tried anything new.
Albert Einstein

If only your goal is to become rich, you will never achieve it.
John D. Rockefeller

Most people spend more time and energy going around problems than in trying to solve them.
Henry Ford

The only real mistake is the one from which we learn nothing.
John Powell

If you don't make mistakes, you aren't really trying.
Coleman Hawkins

The greatest mistake a man can make is to be afraid of making one.
Elbert Hubbard

Our greatest glory is not in never falling, but in rising every time we fall.
Confucius

Don't fear failure. Not failure, but low aim, is the crime. In great attempts it is glorious even to fail.
Bruce Lee

By failing to prepare, you are preparing to fail.
Benjamin Franklin

If I find 10,000 ways something won't work, I haven't failed. I am not discouraged, because every wrong attempt discarded is often a step forward.
Thomas Edison

Failure is nature's plan to prepare you for great responsibilities.
Napoleon Hill

All men make mistakes, but only wise men learn from their mistakes.
Winston Churchill

I love fools experiments. I am always making them.
Charles Darwin

Try and fail, but don't fail to try.
Stephen Kaggwa

Winners lose more than losers. They win and lose more than losers because they stay in the game.
Terry Paulson

All businesses make mistakes. The trick is to avoid large ones.
Carlosslim

I have always tried to turn every disaster into an opportunity.
John D. Rockefeller

Speed is useful only if you are running in the right direction.
Joel Barker

Chapter: Product

The ability of a successful company to add functionality to its product has long been upheld.
Bill Gates

Every day that we spent not improving our products was a wasted day.
Joel Spolsky

Global vision, local win.
Jack Ma

It's more effective to do something valuable than to hope a logo or name will say it for you.
Jason Cohen

I try to keep the meetings small, especially when we're doing product design.
Justin Kan

The secret of creativity is knowing how to hide your sources
Albert Einstein

A market is never saturated with a good product, but it is very quickly saturated with a bad one .
Henry Ford

Make it simple. Make it memorable. Make it inviting to look at. Make it fun to read.
Leo Burnett

Human nature has a tendency to admire complexity but reward simplicity.
Ben Huh

Quality is more important than quantity. One home run is much better than two doubles.
Steve Jobs

You can hype a questionable product for a little while, but you'll never build an enduring business.
Victor Kiam

Every business and every product has risks. You can't get around it.
Lee Iacocca

Don't be afraid to give up the good to go for the great.
John D. Rockefeller

Chapter : Customer

The customer has always driven the business model…
Amancio Ortega Gaona

Your most unhappy customers are your greatest source of learning.
Bill Gates

Wonder what your customer really wants? Ask. Don't tell.
Lisa Stone

If I asked my customers what they wanted they would have said a faster horse.
Henry Ford

Without customers, you don't have a business. You have a hobby.
Don Peppers & Martha Rogers

There is only one boss – the customer. And he can fire everybody in the company from the chairman on down, simply by spending his money somewhere else.
Sam Walton

The purpose of a business is to create a customer.
Peter Drucker

Clients don't care about the labor pains; they want to see the baby.
Tim Williams

Rule 1: The customer is always right. Rule 2: If the customer is ever wrong, re-read Rule 1.
Stew Leonard

If you make customers unhappy in the physical world, they might each tell 6 friends. If you make customers unhappy on the Internet, they can each tell 6,000 friends.
Jeff Bezos

Here is a simple but powerful rule: always give people more than what they expect to get.
Nelson Boswell

No man is an island, entire of itself; every man is a piece of the continent.
John Donne

Individual commitment to a group effort--that is what makes a team work, a company work, a society work, a civilization work.
Vince Lombardi

Coming together is a beginning. Keeping together is progress. Working together is success.
Henry Ford

The strength of the team is each individual member. The strength of each member is the team.
Phil Jackson

Talent wins games, but teamwork and intelligence wins championships.
Michael Jordan

Teamwork is the ability to work together toward a common vision. The ability to direct individual accomplishments toward organizational objectives. It is the fuel that allows common people to attain uncommon results.
Andrew Carnegie

Alone we can do so little, together we can do so much.
Helen Keller

Remember teamwork begins by building trust. And the only way to do that is to overcome our need for invulnerability.
Patrick Lencioni

I invite everyone to choose forgiveness rather than division, teamwork over personal ambition.
Jean-Francois Cope

The best teamwork comes from men who are working independently toward one goal in unison.
James Cash Penney

Teamwork is the secret that makes common people achieve uncommon results.
Ifeanyi Onuoha

A successful team is a group of many hands but of one mind.
Bill Bethel

It is better to have one person working with you than three people working for you.
Dwight D. Eisenhower

A major reason capable people fail to advance, is that they do not work well with their colleagues.
Lee Iacocca

No one can whistle a symphony. It takes an orchestra to play it.
H.E. Luccock

A group becomes a team when each member is sure enough of himself and his contribution to praise the skill of the others.
Norman S Hidle

It is literally true that you can succeed best and quickest by helping others to succeed.
Napoleon Hill

A single arrow is easily broken, but not ten in a bundle.
Japanese Proverb

If you don't kick things around with people, you are out of it. Nobody, I always say, can be anybody without somebody being around.
John Wheeler

All of us, at certain moments of our lives, need to take advice and to receive help from other people.
Alexis Carrel

Individually we are one drop.
Together we are an ocean.
Ryunosuke Satoro

Team means Together Everyone Achieves More!
Proverb

A team is more than a collection of people. It is a process of give and take.
- Barbara Glacel & Emile Robert Jr.

One man can be a crucial ingredient on a team, but one man cannot make a team.
Kareem Abdul-Jabbor

Finding good players is easy. Getting them to play as a team is another story.
Casey Stengel

Trust is knowing that when a team member does push you, they're doing it because they care about the team.
PatrickLencioni

If a team is to reach its potential, each player must be willing to subordinate his personal goals to the good of the team. Bud Wilkinson

Bad attitudes will ruin your team.
Terry Bradshaw

Together, ordinary people can achieve extraordinary results.
Becka Schoettle

Without forgiveness, there can be no real freedom to act within a group.
Max DePree

Group desire is different than individual desire. With individual desire, it's up to you to feed the fire. With group desire, you get all kinds of people rolling logs on from every direction.
Vince Pfaff

No man becomes rich unless he enriches others.
Andrew Carnegie

A group is a bunch of people in an elevator. A team is also a bunch of people in an elevator, but the elevator is broken!
Bonnie Edelstein

Chapter: Leadership

As we look ahead into the next century, leaders will be those who empower others.
Bill Gates

As a leader, one should spend more time than others planning for the future.
Li Ka Shing

A good objective of leadership is to help those who are doing poorly to do well and to help those who are doing well to do even better.
Jim Rohn

I start with the premise that the function of leadership is to produce more leaders, not more followers.
Ralph Nader

A leader must inspire or his team will expire.
Orrin Woodward

A person who is quietly confident makes the best leader.
Fred Wilson

Always treat your employees exactly as you want them to treat your best customers.
Stephen R. Covey

People ask the difference between a leader and a boss. The leader works in the open, and the boss in covert. The leader leads, and the boss drives.
Theodore Roosevelt

Leadership is influence.
John C. Maxwell

Good leaders must first become good servants.
Robert Greenleaf

First humbly serve others then lead them.
Li Ka Shing

A genuine leader is not a searcher for consensus, but a molder of consensus.
Martin Luther King

The challenge of leadership is to be strong, but not rude; be kind, but not weak; be bold, but not bully; be thoughtful, but not lazy; be humble, but not timid; be proud, but not arrogant; have humor, but without folly.
Jim Rohn

Outstanding leaders go out of their way to boost the self-esteem of their personnel. If people believe in themselves, it's amazing what they can accomplish.
Sam Walton

A leader is one who knows the way, goes the way, and shows the way. –
John C. Maxwell

Managers tell you where you are, leaders tell you where you"re going.
Rands

A good leader inspires people to have confidence in the leader, a great leader inspires people to have confidence in themselves
Eleanor Roosevelt

Innovation distinguishes between a leader and a follower
Steve Jobs

I have always found that the speed of the boss is the speed of the team.
Lee Iacocca

If your actions inspire others to dream more, learn more, do more and become more, you are a leader.
John Quincy Adams

Leadership is a potent combination of strategy and character. But if you must be without one, be without the strategy.
Norman Schwarzkopf

Leadership does not depend on being right.
Ivan Illich

The first responsibility of a leader is to define reality. The last is to say thank you. In between, the leader is a servant.
Max DePree

The growth and development of people is the highest calling of leadership.
Harvey Firestone

Leaders think and talk about the solutions. Followers think and talk about the problems.
Brian Tracy

The greatest leader is not necessarily the one who does the greatest things. He is the one that gets the people to do the greatest things.
Ronald Reagan

You manage things; you lead people.
Rear Admiral Grace Murray Hopper

Great leaders are almost always great simplifiers, who can cut through argument, debate, and doubt to offer a solution everybody can understand.
General Colin Powell

A leader is a dealer in hope.
Napoleon Bonaparte

Management is doing things right; leadership is doing the right things.
Peter F. Drucker

A leader is one who sees more than others see, who sees farther than others see, and who sees before others see.
Leroy Eimes

To lead people, walk behind them.
Lao Tzu

Good leadership consists of showing average people how to do the work of superior people.
John D. Rockefeller

We need to move from the leader as hero, to the leader as host.

Margaret Wheatley

The pessimist complains about the wind. The optimist expects it to change. The leader adjusts the sails.
John Maxwell

Leadership: the art of getting someone else to do something you want done because he wants to do it.
Dwight Eisenhower

Don't tell people how to do things, tell them what to do and let them surprise you with their results.
George S. Patton

Sometimes, I think my most important job as a CEO is to listen for bad news. If you don't act on it, your people will eventually stop bringing bad news to your attention and that is the beginning of the end.
Bill Gates

Chapter: Worker- Wages-Bank-Capital

Well-spent aid money is saving lives for a few thousand dollars per life saved.
Bill Gates

If you buy things you do not need, soon you will have to sell things you need.
Warren Buffett

Do not save what is left after spending, but spend what is left after saving.
Warren Buffett

Recessions are great because they unlock the best people.
Aaron Patzer

The secret to successful hiring is this: look for the people who want to change the world.
Marc Benioff

The cost of hiring someone bad is so much greater than missing out on someone good.
Joe Kraus

I would rather earn 1% off a 100 people's efforts than 100% of my own efforts.
John D. Rockefeller

The secret of success lies not in doing your own work, but in recognizing the right man to do it.
Andrew Carnegie

The average person puts only 25% of his energy and ability into his work. The world takes off its hat to those who put in more than 50% of their capacity, and stands on its head for those few and far between souls who devote 100%.
Andrew Carnegie

I don't want a nation of thinkers, I want a nation of workers.
John D. Rockefeller

Honesty is very expensive gift. Do not expect it from cheap people.
Warren Buffett

The art of good management lies in the capacity to accept change, and the ability to meld new and traditional thinking. Successful managers should also have a keen eye for talent. They not only select people who are smarter than themselves, but also avoid picking corporate superstars whose reputation precedes them.
Li Ka Shing

It's not the employer who pays the wages. Employers only handle the money. It's the customer who pays the wages.
Henry Ford

Most people work just hard enough not to get fired and get paid just enough money not to quit.
George Carlin

A bank is a place that will lend you money if you can prove that you don't need it.
Bob Hope

Banks have a new image. Now you have 'a friend,' your friendly banker. If the banks are so friendly, how come they chain down the pens?
Alan King

I believe that banking institutions are more dangerous to our liberties than standing armies.
Thomas Jefferson

Let me issue and control a nation's money and I care not who writes the laws.
Mayer Amschel Rothschild

It is well enough that people of the nation do not understand our banking and money system, for if they did, I believe there would be a revolution before tomorrow morning.
Henry Ford

The highest use of capital is not to make more money, but to make money do to more for the betterment of life.
Henry Ford

Sweat equity is the best startup capital.
Mark Cuban

Always invest for the long term.
Warren Buffett

Diversification may preserve wealth, but concentration builds wealth.
Warren Buffett

Chapter: Investment

There is no magic chart or statistic for investing.
Warren Buffett

On the other hand, investing is a unique kind of casino—one where you cannot lose in the end, so long as you play only by the rules that put the odds squarely in your favor.
Benjamin Graham

Wide diversification is only required when investors do not understand what they are doing.
Warren Buffett

The underlying principles of sound investment should not alter from decade to decade, but the application of these principles must be adapted to significant changes in the financial mechanisms and climate.
Benjamin Graham

Well, when I was very young, maybe 12 years, I began to make investments.
Carlos Slim

The investors should know about these possibilities [Shares going up and down] and should be prepared for them both financially and psychologically. He will want to benefit from changes in market levels – certainly through an advance in the value of his stock holdings as time goes on, and perhaps also by making purchases and sales at advantageous prices. This interest on his part is inevitable and legitimate enough. But it involves the very real danger that it will lead him into speculative attitudes and activities.
Benjamin Graham

Rule No.1: Never lose money. Rule No.2: Never forget rule No.1.
Warren Buffett

To make a million, start with $900,000.
Morton Shulman.

Wide diversification is only required when investors do not understand what they are doing.
Warren Buffett

Investing should be more like watching paint dry or watching grass grow. If you want excitement, take $800 and go to Las Vegas.
Paul Samuelson

Sometimes your best investments are the ones you don't make.
Donald Trump

Great investment opportunities come around when excellent companies are surrounded by unusual circumstances that cause the stock to be misappraised.
Warren Buffett

The way to become rich is to put all your eggs in one basket and then watch that basket.
Andrew Carnegie

We are convinced that the average investor cannot deal successfully with price movements by endeavouring to forecast them.
Benjamin Graham

We also get thousands of suggestions. The default answer is always no.
Jason Fried

The only question with wealth is what you do with it.
John D. Rockefeller

An investment operation is one which, upon thorough analysis, promises safety of principal and an adequate return. Operations not meeting these requirements are speculative.
Benjamin Graham

Know what you own, and know why you own it.
Peter Lynch

Investment is most intelligent when it is most businesslike.
Benjamin Graham

An investment in knowledge pays the best interest.
Benjamin Franklin

The individual investor should act consistently as an investor and not as a speculator. This means that he should be able to justify every purchase he makes and each price he pays by impersonal, objective reasoning that satisfies him that he is getting more than his money's worth for his purchase.
Benjamin Graham

As a speculator you must embrace disorder and chaos.
Louis Bacon

It remained true that sound investment principles produced generally sound results.
Benjamin Graham

I don't want a lot of good investments; I want a few outstanding ones.
Philip Fisher

Never invest in a business you cannot understand.
Warren Buffett

The four most dangerous words in investing are: 'this time it's different'.
John Templeton

Time is your friend; impulse is your enemy.
John Bogle

The investor's chief problem – and even his worst enemy – is likely to be himself.
Benjamin Graham

I never attempt to make money on the stock market. I buy on the assumption that they could close the market the next day and not reopen it for ten years.
Warren Buffett

Price is what you pay; value is what you get.
Warren Buffett

With every new wave of optimism or pessimism, we are ready to abandon history and time-tested principles; but we cling tenaciously and unquestioningly to our prejudices.
Benjamin Graham

I do not like debt and do not like to invest in companies that have too much debt, particularly long-term debt. With long-term debt, increases in interest rates can drastically affect company profits and make future cash flows less predictable.
Warren Buffett

This company looks cheap, that company looks cheap, but the overall economy could completely screw it up. The key is to wait. Sometimes the hardest thing to do is to do nothing.
David Tepper

The most realistic distinction between the investor and the speculator is found in their attitude toward stock-market movements. The speculator's primary interest lies in anticipating and profiting from market fluctuations. The investors primary interest lies in acquiring and holding suitable securities at suitable prices.
Benjamin Graham

Whether we're talking about socks or stocks, I like buying quality merchandise when it is marked down.
Warren Buffett

To achieve satisfactory investment results is easier than most people realize; to achieve superior results is harder than it looks.
Benjamin Graham

Read Ben Graham and Phil Fisher read annual reports, but don't do equations with Greek letters in them.
Warren Buffett

He believed in cash. He did not like companies that had a lot of bonds.
Irving Khan

Most people get interested in stocks when everyone else is. The time to get interested is when no one else is. You can't buy what is popular and do well.
Warren Buffett

The one principal that applies to nearly all these so-called "technical approaches" is that one should buy because a stock or the market has gone up and one should sell because it has declined. This is the exact opposite of sound business sense everywhere else, and it is most unlikely that it can lead to lasting success in Wall Street. In our own stock-market experience and observation, extending over 50 years, we have not known a single person who has consistently or lastingly made money by thus "following the market." We do not hesitate to declare that this approach is as fallacious as it is popular.
Benjamin Graham

I try to buy stock in businesses that are so wonderful that an idiot can run them. Because sooner or later, one will.
Warren Buffett

It has long been the prevalent view that the art of successful investment lies first in the choice of those industries that are most likely to grow in the future and then in identifying the most promising companies in these industries.
Benjamin Graham

If a business does well, the stock eventually follows.
Warren Buffett

I'm only rich because I know when I'm wrong…I basically have survived by recognizing my mistakes.
George Soros

First of all I trust my own instinct, experience that I gained over years and feeling when the moment is right for buying shares. That is what one calls intuition.
Alisher Usmanov

It's not whether you're right or wrong that's important, but how much money you make when you're right and how much you lose when you're wrong.
George Soros

Let blockheads read what blockheads wrote.
Warren Buffett

I haven't met a rich technician.
Jim Rogers

Nine statistical requirements: 1) Adequate size 2) A sufficiently strong financial condition 3) Continued dividends for at least the past 20 years 4) No earnings deficit in the past ten years (No loss) 5) Ten year growth of at least one third in per-share earnings 6) Price of stock no more than 1.5 times net asset value 7) Price no more than 15 times average earnings of the past three years.
Benjamin Graham

Even a mere lack of interest or enthusiasm may impel a price decline to absurdly low levels. Thus we have what appear to be two major sources or undervaluation: 1) currently disappointing results and 2) protracted neglect or unpopularity.
Benjamin Graham

Even with a margin [of safety] in the investor's favor, an individual security may work out badly. For the margin guarantees only that he has a better chance for profit than for loss - not that loss is impossible. But as the number of such commitments is increased the more certain does it become that the aggregate of the profits will exceed the aggregate of the losses.
Benjamin Graham

Chapter: Risk - Market

Risk comes from not knowing what you're doing.
Warren Buffett

There is no such thing as high returns without risk.
Gerry Schwartz

If you have trouble imaging a 20% loss in the stock market, you shouldn't be in stocks.
John Bogle

Risk can be greatly reduced by concentrating on only a few holdings.
Warren Buffett

Never test the depth of river with both the feet.
Warren Buffett

You can not control the market you can not predict the market you can control only two things: this is you and your risk.
Birger Schafermeier

In the short run, the market is a voting machine, but in the long run it is a weighing machine.
Benjamin Graham

Every once in a while, the market does something so stupid it takes your breath away.
Jim Cramer

Look at market fluctuations as your friend rather than your enemy; profit from folly rather than participate in it.
Warren Buffett

Don't look for the needle in the haystack. Just buy the haystack!
Jack Bogle

A prediction about the direction of the stock market tells you nothing about where stocks are headed, but a whole lot about the person doing the predicting.
Warren Buffett

The market is fond of making mountains out of molehills and exaggerating ordinary vicissitudes [A change of circumstances or fortune] into major setbacks.
Benjamin Graham

Only buy something that you'd be perfectly happy to hold if the market shut down for 10 years.
Warren Buffett

Price fluctuations have only one significant meaning for the true investor. They provide him with an opportunity to buy wisely when prices fall sharply and to sell wisely when they advance a great deal. At other times he will do better if he forgets about the stock market and pays attention to his dividend returns and to the operating results of his companies.
Benjamin Graham

Wall Street is the only place that people ride to in a Rolls-Royce to get advice from those who take the subway.
Warren Buffett

The stock market is filled with individuals who know the price of everything, but the value of nothing.
Philip Fisher

It is the new and different that is always most vulnerable to market research.
Malcolm Gladwell

It's tough when markets change and your people within the company don't.
Harvard Business

If you're in business, you need to understand the environment. You need to have a vision of the future, and you need to know the past.
Carlosslim

Competition makes you better, always, always makes you better, even if the competitor wins.
Carlosslim

Chapter: Reputation

Reputation is the key to success. You have to be loyal to your customers.
Li Ka Shing

The reason I became successful is because I touched. I touched my community.
Gary Vaynerchuk

If you have a strong, loyal community, you can do anything.
Jacob Dehart

A good reputation for yourself and your company is an invaluable asset not reflected in the balance sheets.
Li Ka Shing

The purest treasure mortal times can afford is a spotless reputation.
William Shakespeare

The most important thing for a young man is to establish a credit, a reputation, character.
John D. Rockefeller

Think like a wise man but communicate in the language of the people
William Butler Yeats

Next to doing the right thing, is to let people know you are doing the right thing.
John D. Rockefeller

It doesn't matter how strong or capable you are; if you don't have a big heart, you will not succeed.
Li Ka Shing

Chapter: Marketing

The aim of marketing is to know and understand the customer so well the product or service fits him and sells itself.
Peter F. Drucker

The urgent can drown out the important.
Marissa Mayer

Business has only two functions – marketing and innovation.
Milan Kundera

Don't find customers for your products, find products for your customers.
Seth Godin

Increasingly, mass marketing is turning into a mass of niches.
Chris Anderson

Marketing takes a day to learn. Unfortunately it takes a lifetime to master.
Phil Kolter

Advertising in the final analysis should be news. If it is not news it is worthless.
Adolph Ochs

Man's mind, once stretched by a new idea, never regains its original dimensions
Oliver Wendell Holmes

Clarity trumps persuasion.
DR.Flint

Try not to become a man of success but rather a man of value.
Albert Einstein

Advertising is a tax for having an unremarkable product.
Robert Stephens

Customers can't always tell you what they want, but they can always tell you what's wrong.

Carly Fiona

Many a small thing has been made large by the right kind of advertising.
Mark Twain

If you don't believe in your product, or if you're not consistent and regular in the way you promote it, the odds of succeeding go way down. The primary function of the marketing plan is to ensure that you have the resources and the wherewithal to do what it takes to make your product work.
Jay Levinson

You can't just ask customers what they want and then try to give that to them. By the time you get it built, they'll want something new.
Steve Jobs

Make the customer the hero of your story.
Ann Handley

Give them quality, that's the best kind of advertising
Milton Hershey

In marketing I've seen only one strategy that can't miss - and that is to market to your best customers first, your best prospects second and the rest of the world last.
John Romero

Marketing is what you do when your product is no good.
Edwin Land

Chapter : Brand

People build brands the way birds build nests. Through the straws and scraps they chance upon.
Jeremy Bullmore

Your culture is your brand.
Tony Hsieh

Your premium brand had better been delivering something special, or it's not going to get the business.
Warren Buffett

If you are not a brand, you are a commodity.
Philip Kotler

Either write something worth reading or do something worth writing about.
Benjamin Franklin

Brand is not a product, that's for sure; it's not one item. It's an idea, it's a theory, it's a meaning, it's how you carry yourself. It's aspirational, it's inspirational.
Kevin Plank

Brand is just a perception, and perception will match reality over time. Sometimes it will be ahead, other times it will be behind. But brand is simply a collective impression some have about a product.
Elon Musk

A brand is a voice and a product is a souvenir.
Lisa Gansky

Chapter: Plan and Strategy

The essence of strategy is choosing what not to do.
Michael E. Porter

The key factor in my strategy is longevity.
Sheldon Adelson

However beautiful the strategy, you should occasionally look at the results.
Winston Churchill

Victorious warriors win first and then go to war, while defeated warriors go to war first and then seek to win.
Sun Tzu

The best CEOs I know are teachers, and at the core of what they teach is strategy.
Michael Porter

What business strategy is all about-what distinguishes it from all other kinds of business planning-is, in a word, competitive advantage. Without competitors there would be no need for strategy, for the sole purpose of strategic planning is to enable the company to gain, as efficiently as possible, a sustainable edge over its competitors.
Kenichi Ohmae

Strategy without tactics is the slowest route to victory. Tactics without strategy is the noise before defeat.
Sun Tzu

Sound strategy starts with having the right goal.
Michael Porter

The real challenge in crafting strategy lies in detecting subtle discontinuities that may undermine a business in the future. And for that there is no technique, no program, just a sharp mind in touch with the situation.
Henry Mintzberg

Strategy is not the consequence of planning, but the opposite: its starting point.

Henry Mintzberg

If you can't describe your strategy in twenty minutes, simply and in plain language, you haven't got a plan. 'But,' people may say, 'I've got a complex strategy. It can't be reduced to a page.' That's nonsense. That's not a complex strategy. It's a complex thought about the strategy.
Larry Bossidy

The company without a strategy is willing to try anything.
Michael Porter

In real life, strategy is actually very straightforward. You pick a general direction and implement like hell.
Jack Welch

Strategy is not a solo sport, even if you're the CEO.
Max McKeown

What's the use of running if you are not on the right road.
German proverb

Chapter: Service- Firm- Profit

Always deliver more than expected.
Larry Page

It's very easy to be different, but very difficult to be better.
Jonathan Ive

It's not enough that we do our best; sometimes we have to do what's required.
Winston Churchill

We all know that products don't drive sales—people do. We buy the person, not the service.
Jarod Kintz

If you want a successful business, your people must feel that you are working for them—not that they are working for you.
Sam Walton

If you do build a great experience, customers tell each other about that. Word of mouth is very powerful.
Jeff Bezos

It is not the strongest of the species that survives, nor the most intelligent, but the one most responsive to change.
Charles Darwin

Quality in a service or product is not what you put into it. It is what the client or customer gets out of it.
Peter Drucker

If you keep your eye on the profit, you're going to skimp on the product. But if you focus on making really great products, then the profits will follow."
Steve Jobs

In the end, all business operations can be reduced to three words: people, product, and profits.
Lee Iacocca

Profit is not the legitimate purpose of business. The legitimate purpose of business is to provide a product or service that people need and do it so well that it's profitable.
James Rouse

He profits, most who serves best.
F. Sheldon

People should only profit to the extent they make other peoples lives better.
Charles Koch

Honesty is the most single most important factor having a direct bearing on the final success of an individual, corporation, or product.
Ed McMahon

I think that it's always possible to have a great company if you have great ideas.
Jerry Yang

The role of business is to provide products and services that make people's lives better - while using fewer resources - and to act lawfully and with integrity.
Charles Koch

Time is the friend of the wonderful company, the enemy of the mediocre.
Warren Buffett

Chapter: Think

Communication: first seek common ground then seek the differences.
Entrepreneurship: first make it grows then make it a success.
Workplace: first raise your value then be promoted.
Excution: first complete it then perfect it.
Learning: first write it down then remember it.
Design: first imitate then innovate.
Interpersonal relationship: first exchange ideas then engage the hearts.
Development: first make it stand then make it tall.
First do well ourselves then demand on others.
First handle the emotions then solve the issues.
First prepare well then gain great success.
First judge ourselves then we can judge others.
First establish oneself then seek to forget oneself.
Li Ka Shing

If you can't do a thing better than others are doing it, don't do it at all.
Philip Fisher

Just do things different.
Sheldon Adelson

I'm addicted to winning. The more you win, the more you want to win.
Larry Ellison

Someone's sitting in the shade today because someone planted a tree a long
time ago.
Warren Buffett

I knew a lot about what I did when I was 20. I had read a lot, and I aspired to
learn everything I could about the subject.
Warren Buffett

The business schools reward complex behavior more than simple behavior,
but simple behavior is more effective.
Warren Buffett

I wasn't lucky. I worked hard to achieve the goals I set for myself.
Li Ka Shing

Enjoy your work and work for whom you admire.
Warren Buffett

Never give up searching for the job that you're passionate about. Try to find the job you'd have if you were independently rich. Forget about the pay. When you're associating with the people that you love, doing what you love, it doesn't get any better than that.
Warren Buffett

Nothing is worth doing unless it is worth doing right.
Philip Fisher

1. Bill Gates

William Henry "Bill" Gates III (born October 28, 1955) is an American business magnate, philanthropist, investor, computer programmer, and inventor.Gates is the former chief executive and chairman of Microsoft, the world's largest personal-computer software company, which he co-founded with Paul Allen.

He is consistently ranked in the Forbes list of the world's wealthiest people and was the wealthiest overall from 1995 to 2009—excluding 2008, when he was ranked third;in 2011 he was the wealthiest American and the world's second wealthiest person. According to the Bloomberg Billionaires List, Gates became the world's richest person again in May 2013, a position that he last held on the list in 2007. He held the position until Carlos Slim reclaimed it in July 2014.As of September 2014, he is the second richest person in the world.

2. Warren Buffett

Warren Edward Buffett (born August 30, 1930) is an American business magnate, investor and philanthropist. He was the most successful investor of the 20th century. Buffett is the chairman, CEO and largest shareholder of Berkshire Hathaway, and consistently ranked among the world's wealthiest people. He was ranked as the world's wealthiest person in 2008 and as the third wealthiest in 2011. In 2012 Time named Buffett one of the world's most influential people.

Buffett is called the "Wizard of Omaha" or "Oracle of Omaha", or the "Sage of Omaha" and is noted for his adherence to value investing and for his personal frugality despite his immense wealth. Buffett is a notable philanthropist, having pledged to give away 99 percent of his fortune to philanthropic causes, primarily via the Gates Foundation.

3. Henry Ford

Henry Ford (July 30, 1863 – April 7, 1947) was an American industrialist, the founder of the Ford Motor Company, and sponsor of the development of the assembly line technique of mass production. Although Ford did not invent the automobile or the assembly line, he developed and manufactured the first automobile that many middle class Americans could afford.

In doing so, Ford converted the automobile from an expensive curiosity into a practical conveyance that would profoundly impact the landscape of the twentieth century. His introduction of the Model T automobile revolutionized transportation and American industry. As owner of the Ford Motor Company, he became one of the richest and best-known people in the world. He is credited with "Fordism": mass production of inexpensive goods coupled with high wages for workers. Ford had a global vision, with consumerism as the key to peace. His intense commitment to systematically lowering costs resulted in many technical and business innovations, including a franchise system that put dealerships throughout most of North America and in major cities on six continents.

Ford left most of his vast wealth to the Ford Foundation and arranged for his family to control the company permanently. Ford was also widely known for his pacifism during the first years of World War I, and also for being the publisher of antisemitic texts such as the book The International Jew.

4. John Davidson Rockefeller

John Davison Rockefeller, Sr. (July 8, 1839 – May 23, 1937) was an American business magnate and philanthropist. He was a co-founder of the Standard Oil Company, which dominated the oil industry and was the first great U.S. business trust. Rockefeller revolutionized the petroleum industry, and along with other key contemporary industrialists such as Andrew Carnegie, defined the structure of modern philanthropy. In 1870, he co-founded Standard Oil Company and actively ran it until he officially retired in 1897.

Rockefeller founded Standard Oil as an Ohio partnership with his brother William along with Henry Flagler, Jabez A. Bostwick, chemist Samuel Andrews, and a silent partner, Stephen V. Harkness. As kerosene and gasoline grew in importance, Rockefeller's wealth soared and he became the world's richest man and the first American worth more than a billion dollars. Adjusting for inflation, he is often regarded as the richest person in history.

Rockefeller spent the last 40 years of his life in retirement at his estate, Kykuit, in Westchester County, New York. His fortune was mainly used to create the modern systematic approach of targeted philanthropy. He was able to do this through the creation of foundations that had a major effect on medicine, education and scientific research. His foundations pioneered the development of medical research and were instrumental in the eradication of hookworm and yellow fever.

Rockefeller was also the founder of both the University of Chicago and Rockefeller University and funded the establishment of Central Philippine University in the Philippines. He was a devoted Northern Baptist and supported many church-based institutions. Rockefeller adhered to total abstinence from alcohol and tobacco throughout his life. He was a faithful congregant of the Erie Street Baptist Mission Church, where he taught Sunday school, and served as a trustee, clerk, and occasional janitor. Religion was a guiding force throughout his life, and Rockefeller believed it to be the source of his success. Rockefeller was also considered a supporter of capitalism based in a perspective of social darwinism, and is often quoted saying "The growth of a large business is merely a survival of the fittest".

5. Andrew Carnegie

Andrew Carnegie (November 25, 1835 – August 11, 1919) was a Scottish American industrialist who led the enormous expansion of the American steel industry in the late 19th century. He was also one of the highest profile philanthropists of his era and had given away almost 90 percent – amounting to, in 1919, $350 million (in 2014, $4.76 billion) – of his fortune to charities and foundations by the time of his death. His 1889 article proclaiming "The Gospel of Wealth" called on the rich to use their wealth to improve society, and stimulated a wave of philanthropy.

Carnegie was born in Dunfermline, Scotland, and emigrated to the United States with his very poor parents in 1848. Carnegie started as a telegrapher and by the 1860s had investments in railroads, railroad sleeping cars, bridges and oil derricks. He accumulated further wealth as a bond salesman raising money for American enterprise in Europe. He built Pittsburgh's Carnegie Steel Company, which he sold to J.P. Morgan in 1901 for $480 million (in 2014, $13.6 billion), creating the U.S. Steel Corporation.

Carnegie devoted the remainder of his life to large-scale philanthropy, with special emphasis on local libraries, world peace, education and scientific research. With the fortune he made from business, he built Carnegie Hall, and founded the Carnegie Corporation of New York, Carnegie Endowment for International Peace, Carnegie Institution for Science, Carnegie Trust for the Universities of Scotland, Carnegie Hero Fund, Carnegie Mellon University and the Carnegie Museums of Pittsburgh, among others. His life has often been referred to as a true "rags to riches" story.

6. Napoleon Hill

Napoleon Hill (October 26, 1883 – November 8, 1970) was an American author, businessman in the area of the new thought movement who was one of the earliest producers of the modern genre of personal-success literature. He is widely considered to be one of the great writers on success. His most famous work, Think and Grow Rich (1937), is one of the best-selling books of all time (at the time of Hill's death in 1970,

Think and Grow Rich had sold 20 million copies). Hill's works examined the power of personal beliefs, and the role they play in personal success. He became an advisor to President Franklin D. Roosevelt from 1933 to 1936. "Anything the mind of man can conceive and believe, it can achieve," is one of Hill's hallmark expressions. How achievement actually occurs, and a formula for it that puts success in reach of the average person, were the focal points of Hill's books.

7. George Soros

George Soros (born August 12, 1930, as Schwartz György) is a Hungarian-born American business magnate, investor, and philanthropist. He is the chairman of Soros Fund Management. He is known as "The Man Who Broke the Bank of England" because of his short sale of US$10 billion worth of pounds, giving him a profit of $1 billion during the 1992 Black Wednesday UK currency crisis.

Soros is a well-known supporter of progressive-liberal political causes. He played a significant role in the peaceful transition from communism to capitalism in Hungary (1984–89) and provided one of Europe's largest higher education endowments to Central European University in Budapest. Soros is also the chairman of the Open Society Foundations.

8. Steve Jobs

Steven Paul "Steve" Jobs (February 24, 1955 – October 5, 2011) was an American entrepreneur, marketer, and inventor, who was the co-founder, chairman, and CEO of Apple Inc. Through Apple, he is widely recognized as a charismatic and design-driven pioneer of the personal computer revolution and for his influential career in the computer and consumer electronics fields, transforming "one industry after another, from computers and smartphones to music and movies." Jobs also co-founded and served as chief executive of Pixar Animation Studios; he became a member of the board of directors of The Walt Disney Company in 2006, when Disney acquired Pixar. Jobs was among the first to see the commercial potential of Xerox PARC's mouse-driven graphical user interface, which led to the creation of the Apple Lisa and, a year later, the Macintosh. He also played a role in introducing the LaserWriter, one of the first widely available laser printers, to the market.

After a power struggle with the board of directors in 1985, Jobs left Apple and founded NeXT, a computer platform development company specializing in the higher-education and business markets. In 1986, he acquired the computer graphics division of Lucasfilm, which was spun off as Pixar. He was credited in Toy Story (1995) as an executive producer. He served as CEO and majority shareholder until Disney's purchase of Pixar in 2006. In 1996, after Apple had failed to deliver its operating system, Copland, Gil Amelio turned to NeXT Computer, and the NeXTSTEP platform became the foundation for the Mac OS X. Jobs returned to Apple as an advisor, and took control of the company as an interim CEO. Jobs brought Apple from near bankruptcy to profitability by 1998.

As the new CEO of the company, Jobs oversaw the development of the iMac, iTunes, iPod, iPhone, and iPad, and on the services side, the company's Apple Retail Stores, iTunes Store and the App Store. The success of these products and services provided several years of stable financial returns, and propelled Apple to become the world's most valuable publicly traded company in 2011. The reinvigoration of the company is regarded by many commentators as one of the greatest turnarounds in business history.

Jobs received a number of honors and public recognition for his influence in the technology and music industries. He has been referred to as "legendary", a "futurist" and a "visionary", and has been described as the "Father of the Digital Revolution," a "master of innovation," "the master evangelist of the digital age" and a "design perfectionist."

9. Li Ka-shing

Sir Ka-shing Li, GBM, KBE, JP (born 29 July 1928 in Chaozhou, China) is a Hong Kong business magnate, investor, and philanthropist. According to the Bloomberg Billionaires Index, as of April 16, 2014 he is the richest person in Asia, with a net worth of $31.9 billion. He is the Chairman of the Board of Hutchison Whampoa Limited (HWL) and Cheung Kong Holdings as of 2008; through them, he is the world's largest operator of container terminals and the world's largest health and beauty retailer.

Considered one of the most powerful figures in Asia, Li was named "Asia's Most Powerful Man, Li Ka-Ching" by Asiaweek in 2001. His companies make up 15% of the market cap of the Hong Kong Stock Exchange. Forbes Magazine and the Forbes family honoured Li Ka-shing with the first ever "Malcolm S. Forbes Lifetime Achievement Award" on 5 September 2006, in Singapore. In spite of his wealth, Li has cultivated a reputation for leading a no-frills lifestyle, and is known to wear simple black dress shoes and an inexpensive Seiko wristwatch, which is at odds with the house he owns in one of Hong Kong's most expensive precincts, Deep Water Bay in Hong Kong Island. Li is also regarded as one of Asia's most generous philanthropists, donating over US $1.41 billion to date to charity and other various philanthropic causes. Li is often referred to as "Superman" in Hong Kong because of his business prowess. Because of his wealth, he is regarded as a celebrity, and even has a wax statue in his likeness (the only non-artist to have one in Hong Kong).

10. Richard Branson

Sir Richard Charles Nicholas Branson (born 18 July 1950) is an English business magnate and investor. He is best known as the founder of Virgin Group, which comprises more than 400 companies.

At the age of sixteen his first business venture was a magazine called Student. In 1970, he set up a mail-order record business. In 1972, he opened a chain of record stores, Virgin Records, later known as Virgin Megastores. Branson's Virgin brand grew rapidly during the 1980s, as he set up Virgin Atlantic and expanded the Virgin Records music label.

Branson has stated in a number of interviews that he derives much influence from non-fiction books. He most commonly names Nelson Mandela's autobiography, Long Walk to Freedom, explaining that Mandela was "one of the most inspiring men I have ever met and had the honour to call my friend." Owing to his interest in humanitarian and ecological issues, Branson also lists Al Gore's best-selling book, An Inconvenient Truth, and The Revenge of Gaia by James Lovelock amongst his favourites. According to Branson's book, Screw It, Let's do It. Lessons in Life, he is also a huge fan of works by Jung Chang. In terms of fiction, Branson has long held an admiration for the fictional character, Peter Pan, and in 2006 he founded Virgin Comics LLC, stating that Virgin Comics will give "a whole generation of young, creative thinkers a voice."

Source: Wikipedia.org

www.ingramcontent.com/pod-product-compliance
Lightning Source LLC
Chambersburg PA
CBHW050752180526
45159CB00003B/1435